Min Monkey

by Jay Dale

illustrated by Anna Hancock

"Come down,
you **silly** little monkey!"
shouted Grandpa Tut.

"Big Eagle is up in that tree. He looks **hungry** to me!"

"He is not here."

"Come down!"
shouted Grandpa Tut.

"No! No! No!"
said Min Monkey.
"Go away!"

"You are a **silly** little monkey," said Grandpa Tut.

"**Oh, no!**"
said Min Monkey,
and **1, 2, 3** he ran
down that tree.

"Come in here,"
said Grandpa Tut.
"You are
a **silly** little monkey!"